The Christening

Copyright © 2002 John Hunt Publishing Ltd.

Text © 2002 Jacqueline Harding

Illustrations © 2002 Margaret Brampton

ISBN 1 84298 086 6

Designed by
ANDREW MILNE DESIGN

Write to John Hunt Publishing Ltd
46a West Street, Alresford, Hampshire SO24 9AU, UK

The rights of Jacqueline Harding as author and Margaret Brampton as illustrator
of this work have been asserted in accordance with the Copyright,
Designs and Patents Act 1988.

A CIP catalogue record for this book is available from the British Library.

CARE for Education produces educational resources for nursery, primary and
secondary schools, gives guidance and training for teachers and school
governors/board members; facilitates conferences and seminars, and works on
educational policy with Government, local authorities, schools and parents.
Practice and policy work focuses on areas such as early years, school exclusion,
sex and relationships education and school management.

These Early Years books are part of the **Celebrating Marriage** resources
launched in 2001/2. More details of these resources can be found on the
website: www.celebratingmarriage.com

Printed in China

The Christening

Jacqueline Harding

Illustrated by
Margaret Brampton

John Hunt
Publishing Limited

My baby sister called Lola is going to be Christened at our church.

She is still very tiny.

5

During the Christening service the vicar will pray for the baby and sprinkle water on her head.

'It will be a way of thanking God for Lola,' mum said.

Mum and dad are very busy. Lots of people will be coming back to our house for tea after the Christening.

I love helping with the cooking.

Mum and I are going shopping for a dress for Lola to wear at the Christening.

There is only one dress small enough for Lola!

I chose a colourful pair of trousers and top to wear to the Christening.

The day of the Christening arrived.

I've had a shower and changed into my new clothes.

Lola is ready too.

I asked mum for a drink and she poured out a glass of blackcurrant for me.

And, that's when the awful thing happened.

Our cat Fluff's tail swished straight into the drink. The blackcurrant juice went right over the Christening gown!

'Oh no!' said mum.

'Oh Fluff!' I shouted.

Mum tried to get the blackcurrant stain out of the dress, but it wouldn't come out.

'We could run up to the shops and buy another one,' I said.

But mum said they didn't have another one.

'We could make another dress,' I said.

But mum said, 'We haven't got time.'

Then, I ran into the playroom.

Yes! There was a dress just the right size.

'Mum,' I called, 'come here, quickly!'

Mum said the doll's dress was just perfect.

Then, we dashed to the Christening!

This book can be read with children either individually or in groups. Invite the children to think about Christenings.

Have they ever been to a Christening?

It is important to be sensitive and aware that children may have experienced different ceremonies for babies.

You could talk about how each baby is special.

If you were christened as a baby you could show your photos, or, photos of your own children being christened or involved in any other ceremony for babies.

Again, it will be essential to be sensitive to those children whose parents are not married or who have never been christened.